Unlock the Extraordinary Life God Has for You!

Are you ready to embrace the abundant life God intends for you, whether or not "Mr. Right" has come along? This workbook is designed to spark self-reflection, challenge limiting beliefs, and guide you toward personal growth and spiritual renewal. Each question is a step toward discovering your God-given gifts and uncovering the joy that can only come from living a life aligned with Christ's will.

Completing the questions in this workbook will help prepare your heart for the concepts we explore in my book, '**How to Live an Extraordinary Life, With or Without Mr. Right: A Christian Woman's Guide on How to Survive and Thrive on Single Avenue**.' As you dig in, you'll understand who you are, what you value, and how to walk boldly in faith, regardless of your marital status. Don't wait for the future to start living —start now! Your extraordinary life is waiting, and it begins with these questions.

Am I a savvy SINGLE?

Hustle in Faith Inc.
701 Main Street #6003
Evanston, IL 60204
www.withorwithoutmrright.com

First Edition
ISBN 979-8-9917800-4-9

For my beautiful, intelligent amazing mother, Pearlean Johnson. Words cannot begin to express how much you mean to me. The only reason I have been able to live an extraordinary life is due to your unconditional love, courage, resilience and infinite sacrifices. Your constant encouragement is why I continue to soar to new heights. You truly are the wind beneath my wings. I love you! 🤍

Special

Invest

Network

Growth

Light

Educate

Are you ready to embrace your life with or without Mr. Right? Your marital status should not dictate your ability to live the bold, vibrant life you were meant to live. It's time to analyze, apply, and amplify what being a savvy single woman means. This journey isn't about surviving—it's about thriving!

Answering the following questions will clarify who you are, what you desire, and how to create a life filled with purpose, joy, and adventure. Your extraordinary life isn't somewhere out there—it's waiting for *you* to claim it right now. Let's dive in and design a life that reflects your deepest values, passions, and dreams!

SPECIAL

As each one has received a special gift employ it and serving one another as good stewards of the manifold grace of God.
1st Peter 4:10

How do you spend your free time?

What activities bring you joy?

What topics would you love to explore more?

Create a list of all the skills that come easily to you. Write down your experience using those skills.

Think about your most outstanding achievements. What skills did you use to accomplish your goals?

If you are unsure how your skills align with particular occupations, you can take assessments like the Myers-Briggs Type Indicator (MBTI), StrengthsFinder, or DiSC to uncover how your personality and potential talents align. Write down your results. Do you agree or disagree?

Create a mini SWOT of your strengths and weaknesses to see how your skills stack up within your industry.

What are your strengths?

What are your weaknesses?

What opportunities do you believe your skill set can help you achieve?

What are some threats that can prevent you from being successful in using your talent?

Search for opportunities that align with your skills.

INVEST

If any of you lacks wisdom you should ask God who gives generously to all without finding fault and it will be given to you. ~ James 1:5

What workshops, trainings, seminars, or courses will you attend to learn new skills and concepts that align with your talents and career aspirations?

List what books and podcasts will help expand your knowledge.

What newsletters help you stay on top of industry trends and effectively apply your talent?

Identify the thought leaders and industry experts to help in your quest to stay informed.

How will you keep up with the latest trends and technologies?

What challenges do you believe you will encounter?

How will you prepare yourself when you face barriers pushing you outside your comfort zone?

How will you surround yourself with inspiring and motivated individuals?

NETWORK

As iron sharpens iron so one person sharpens another.
~ Proverbs 27:17

Get honest feedback from people who know your strengths.

Engage in new hobbies or activities to discover hidden talents.

Take on new responsibilities or projects at work to test different skills.

Create a list of professional organizations or online communities related to your skills.

Network with professionals in your field at industry events, conferences, and meetups to expand your connections and learn about opportunities to apply your talents.

Collaborate with others on projects that require your talents so you can enhance your skills and learn from each other.

Write a list of accountability groups to share knowledge and challenges.

GROWTH

Practice these things immerse yourself in them so that all may see your progress.
1st Timothy 4:15

What hobbies align with your talents?

Reflect on your performance in different tasks and projects. Are there areas where you can improve?

Regularly review your progress and adjust your approach as needed.

LIGHT

In the same way let your light shine before others that they may see your good deeds and glorify your father in Heaven. ~ Matthew 5:16

Create a personal website to showcase your portfolio, resume, and blog.

Write articles, blogs, or books related to your expertise. Write articles, blogs, or books to share your insights and experiences.

What industry magazines, journals, or online platforms will you write for to reach a wider audience?

What personal projects will you use to develop your talents?

Speak at conferences, seminars, or webinars to share your knowledge. Use public speaking as a platform to demonstrate your expertise and build credibility.

How will you set aside time to practice and refine your skills? Check out this blog post to learn how to create a routine to reign in your lack of direction. https://starengu.com/how-to-reign-in-your-lack-of-direction/

Share your work, insights, and accomplishments on social media platforms. Engage with your audience by posting regularly and participating in discussions.

Enter competitions, contests, or challenges related to your field. Use these opportunities to test your skills, gain recognition, and receive feedback.

EDUCATE

But do not forget to do good and to share for with such sacrifices God is well pleased
~Hebrews 13:16

Offer your talents to local organizations, charities, or community projects. Use your skills to make a positive impact and gain valuable experience.

Take on freelance work or side projects to develop and showcase your talents.

Mentor less experienced individuals in your field.

Are you willing to conduct workshops or training sessions to teach others your skills? Leverage this opportunity to reinforce your knowledge and gain visibility.

What business or side hustle will you start that leverages your talents so you can show off your expertise?

My Career
Playbook

Christian Playbook

Just as athletes use a playbook to help them win the game, a Christian's Playbook is a guide we can reference to ensure we're doing our part to contribute to God's kingdom. The corporate world can be scary if you don't take the time to cultivate the right mindset.

We should take comfort in the fact that God has given us everything we need to succeed. Everyone's playbook will look different, but the outcome will be the same. Answering the following questions will place you in a position to ensure that the corporate world does not devour you.

How will I honor God with the gifts and talents He has given me in my work?

Does my work align with God's purpose for my life?

Regardless of who may be watching, am I operating honestly and transparently?

Are my business practices fair and ethical toward employees, customers, and partners?

Am I a good steward who handles company resources?

Can my employees, coworkers, or clients see Christ in me?

Do I lead with a humble mindset?

Do I encourage a workplace culture of respect, unity, and kindness?

Are my priorities in order (i.e., God, family, etc.)?

Does my work interfere with my relationship with God or others He has placed in my life?

Am I finding ways to rest and recharge, trusting God to sustain me beyond my work?

Do I approach challenges with faith and prayer, seeking God's wisdom first?

When I encounter challenges, do I pray to God, seeking His guidance?

Do I maintain patience and perseverance, trusting in God's timing?

Do I confront those who I believe may have mistreated me or choose to gossip behind their back?

How do I measure success? Am I using the world's ruler or God's ruler?

Am I willing to trust God with my goals and the methods He chooses to manifest those goals?

Am I using my financial blessings to bless others and advance God's kingdom?
How should I view the detours I encounter during my journey?

How can I be a light for Christ in my business or workplace without compromising professionalism?

When opportunities arise, am I open to sharing my faith?

Our lives may be the only "Bible" people read. Am I living a life that inspires them to learn more about Christ?

Do I have mentors or a support system who help me stay grounded in my faith?

Am I open to correction from trusted believers when I stray from God's principles?

Do I seek community with other Christian professionals for mutual encouragement and growth?

Checklist

FAITHPRENEURS RESOURCES

www.hustleinfaith.com

PODCAST

- ☐ Rate this podcast
- ☐ Streamyard
- ☐ Fiverr

VIDEO

- ☐ vidIQ
- ☐ Descript
- ☐ Opus
- ☐ Capcut

MARKETING

- ☐ Grammarly
- ☐ Mailerlite
- ☐ Canva
- ☐ Tailwind

MISC.

- ☐ Siteground
- ☐ Bluchic
- ☐ Audible
- ☐ Redbubble

ARE YOU A GOAL - GETTER?

HEY GOAL-GETTER!

I commend and support your desire to live an extraordinary life. The way to achieve this feat is to ensure that your mind, body, and soul are aligned with God's plans for you.

Discover His plans by devoting time to study His word and using whatever resources you have at your disposal to bet on yourself. This challenge may seem like a daunting task, but believe me, the return on investment is worth the risk.

You got this! 💪

A GOAL WITHOUT A PLAN IS JUST A WISH

It's time to identify your goals and determine what success looks like to you. We're going to create a process to help place you in a position to turn your goals into reality.

Hey Goal-getter!

How many goals did you achieve last year?

If you answered 'none' or 'not many', then you're in the right place! The main reason why people don't achieve their goals is because they don't have a game plan. You can read more about Hustle in Faith's goal-setting system by going to https://hustleinfaith.com/hustle-in-faith-goal-setting-planner-grateful-notes/and completing the below exercises.

Goal #1

S

M

A

R

T

Select one word you can easily associate with your SMART goal.

Goal #1

WRITE DOWN YOUR SMART GOAL

Break down your goal into 3 simple targets:

Target 1

Target 2

Target 3

Action Steps:

Action Steps:

Action Steps:

Goal #2

S

M

A

R

T

Select one word you can easily associate with your SMART goal.

Goal #2

WRITE DOWN YOUR SMART GOAL

Break down your goal into 3 simple targets:

Target 1

Target 2

Target 3

Action Steps:

Action Steps:

Action Steps:

Goal #3

S

M

A

R

T

Select one word you can easily associate with your SMART goal.

Goal #3

WRITE DOWN YOUR SMART GOAL

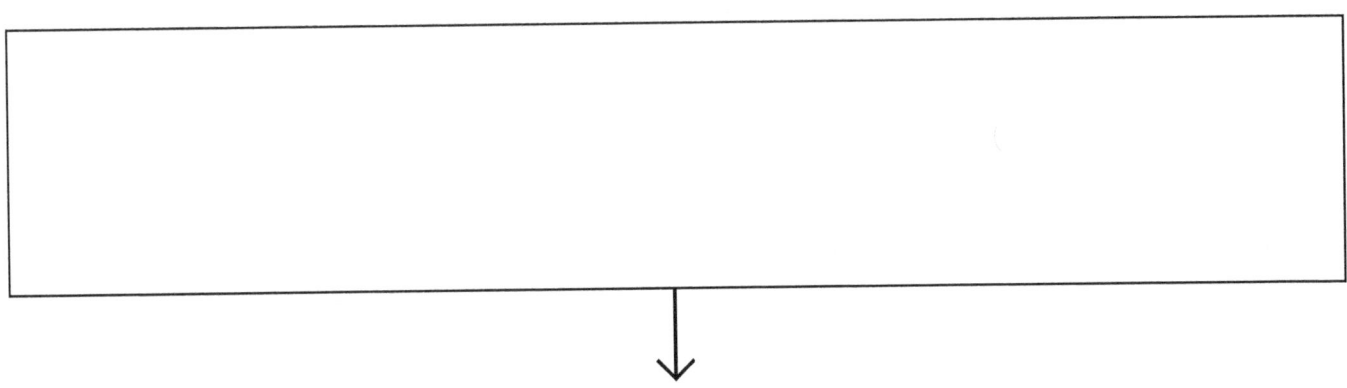

Break down your goal into 3 simple targets:

Target 1	**Target 2**	**Target 3**

Action Steps: Action Steps: Action Steps:

_____   _____   _____

_____   _____   _____

_____   _____   _____

_____   _____   _____

LET'S MAKE IT HAPPEN

"YOUR IMAGINATION IS YOUR PREVIEW OF
LIFE'S COMING ATTRACTIONS."
~ALBERT EINSTEIN

Every day for the next 30 days you will need to
complete the following 3 pages:

Mind

Body

Soul

After 31 days, you will have an opportunity to
see how well you are progressing towards your
goals. Are you ready? Let's go!

MIND

"I the Lord search the heart and examine the mind, to reward each person according to their conduct, according to what their deeds deserve."
~Jer 17:10

HOW DO YOU FEEL?

HOW DID YOU INVEST IN YOURSELF?

BODY

Your eye is the lamp of your body. When your eyes are healthy, your whole body also is full of light. But when they are unhealthy, your body also is full of darkness.
~Luke 11:34

BREAKFAST

SLEEP

QUALITY

TOTAL HOURS

LUNCH

MOOD

WATER

DID I TAKE MY VITAMINS?

YES ☐   NO ☐

WEATHER

SNACKS

EXERCISE

TYPE

TIME

TOTAL STEPS

DINNER

SOUL

What good is it for someone to gain the whole world, yet forfeit their soul?
~Mark 8:36

DID I PRAY?

YES ☐   NO ☐

DID I SPEND TIME WITH GOD?

YES ☐   NO ☐

WHAT AM I GRATEFUL FOR TODAY?

WHAT DID I FEED MY SOUL?

BOOKS

PODCASTS

VERSES

DID I WIN THE BATTLE OF THE MIND?
~2 Cor 10:3-5

**CHOOSE A VERSE THAT RESONATAES WITH YOU.
HOW DOES THIS VERSE APPLY TO YOUR LIFE?**

MIND

"I the Lord search the heart and examine the mind, to reward each person according to their conduct, according to what their deeds deserve."
~Jer 17:10

HOW DO YOU FEEL?

HOW DID YOU INVEST IN YOURSELF?

BODY

Your eye is the lamp of your body. When your eyes are healthy, your whole body also is full of light. But when they are unhealthy, your body also is full of darkness.
~Luke 11:34

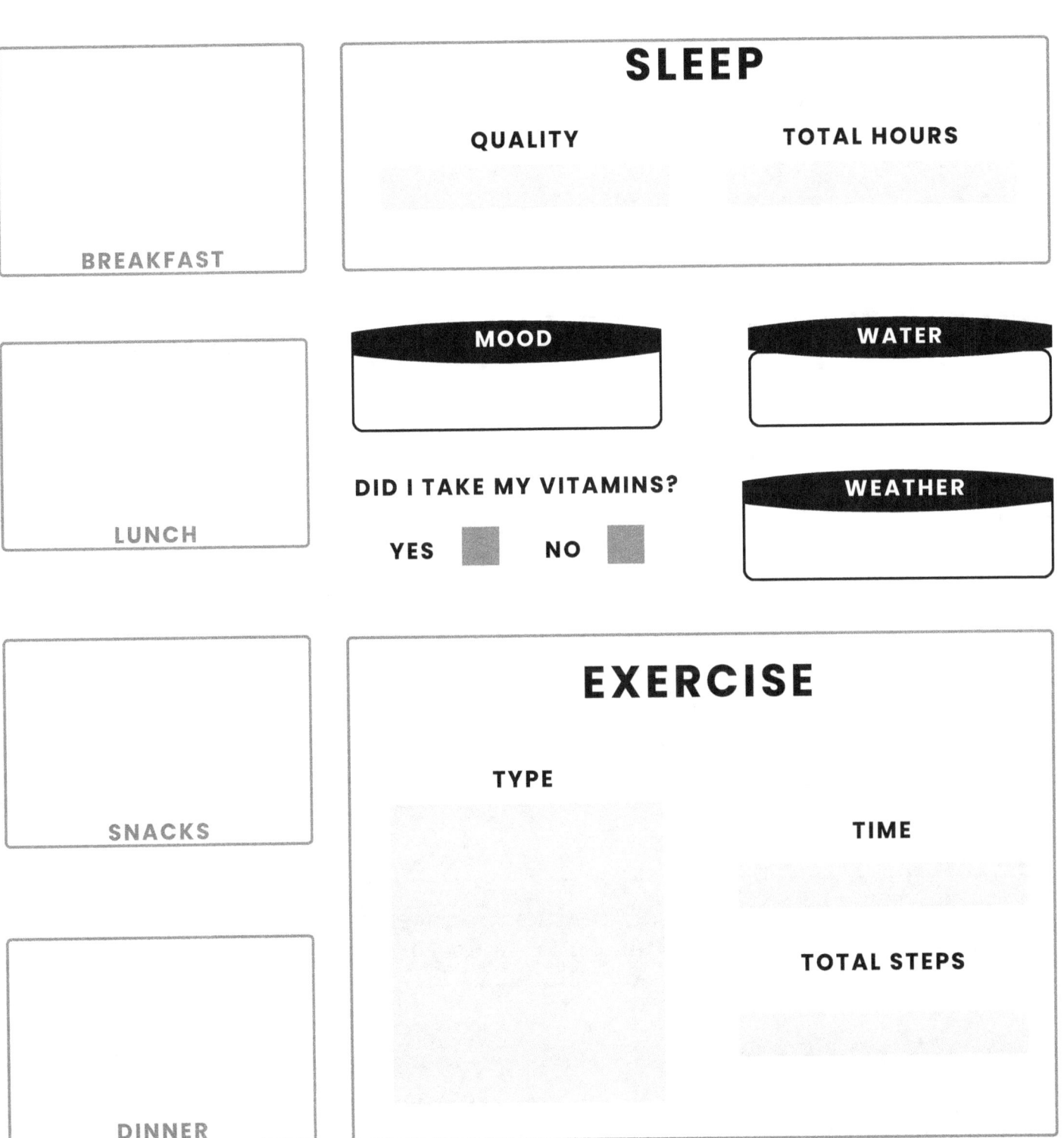

BREAKFAST

SLEEP

QUALITY   TOTAL HOURS

LUNCH

MOOD   WATER

DID I TAKE MY VITAMINS?

YES   NO   WEATHER

SNACKS

EXERCISE

TYPE

TIME

TOTAL STEPS

DINNER

SOUL

What good is it for someone to gain the whole world, yet forfeit their soul?
~Mark 8:36

DID I PRAY?

YES   NO

DID I SPEND TIME WITH GOD?

YES   NO

WHAT AM I GRATEFUL FOR TODAY?

WHAT DID I FEED MY SOUL?

BOOKS	PODCASTS	VERSES

DID I WIN THE BATTLE OF THE MIND?
~2 Cor 10:3-5

CHOOSE A VERSE THAT RESONATAES WITH YOU.
HOW DOES THIS VERSE APPLY TO YOUR LIFE?

MIND

"I the Lord search the heart and examine the mind, to reward each person
according to their conduct, according to what their deeds deserve."
~Jer 17:10

HOW DO YOU FEEL?

HOW DID YOU INVEST IN YOURSELF?

BODY

Your eye is the lamp of your body. When your eyes are healthy, your whole body also is full of light. But when they are unhealthy, your body also is full of darkness.
~Luke 11:34

BREAKFAST

SLEEP

QUALITY   TOTAL HOURS

MOOD

WATER

DID I TAKE MY VITAMINS?

YES   NO

WEATHER

LUNCH

SNACKS

EXERCISE

TYPE

TIME

TOTAL STEPS

DINNER

SOUL

What good is it for someone to gain the whole world, yet forfeit their soul?
~Mark 8:36

DID I PRAY?

YES   NO

DID I SPEND TIME WITH GOD?

YES   NO

WHAT AM I GRATEFUL FOR TODAY?

WHAT DID I FEED MY SOUL?

BOOKS	PODCASTS	VERSES

DID I WIN THE BATTLE OF THE MIND?
~2 Cor 10:3-5

CHOOSE A VERSE THAT RESONATAES WITH YOU.
HOW DOES THIS VERSE APPLY TO YOUR LIFE?

MIND

"I the Lord search the heart and examine the mind, to reward each person according to their conduct, according to what their deeds deserve."
~Jer 17:10

HOW DO YOU FEEL?

HOW DID YOU INVEST IN YOURSELF?

BODY

Your eye is the lamp of your body. When your eyes are healthy, your whole body also is full of light. But when they are unhealthy, your body also is full of darkness.
~Luke 11:34

BREAKFAST

SLEEP

QUALITY

TOTAL HOURS

LUNCH

MOOD

WATER

DID I TAKE MY VITAMINS?

YES ☐ NO ☐

WEATHER

SNACKS

EXERCISE

TYPE

TIME

TOTAL STEPS

DINNER

SOUL

What good is it for someone to gain the whole world, yet forfeit their soul?
~Mark 8:36

DID I PRAY?

YES ☐   NO ☐

DID I SPEND TIME WITH GOD?

YES ☐   NO ☐

WHAT AM I GRATEFUL FOR TODAY?

WHAT DID I FEED MY SOUL?

BOOKS

PODCASTS

VERSES

DID I WIN THE BATTLE OF THE MIND?
~2 Cor 10:3-5

CHOOSE A VERSE THAT RESONATAES WITH YOU.
HOW DOES THIS VERSE APPLY TO YOUR LIFE?

MIND

"I the Lord search the heart and examine the mind, to reward each person according to their conduct, according to what their deeds deserve."
~Jer 17:10

HOW DO YOU FEEL?

HOW DID YOU INVEST IN YOURSELF?

BODY

Your eye is the lamp of your body. When your eyes are healthy, your whole body also is full of light. But when they are unhealthy, your body also is full of darkness.
~Luke 11:34

BREAKFAST

SLEEP

QUALITY

TOTAL HOURS

LUNCH

MOOD

WATER

DID I TAKE MY VITAMINS?

YES [ ]   NO [ ]

WEATHER

SNACKS

EXERCISE

TYPE

TIME

TOTAL STEPS

DINNER

SOUL

What good is it for someone to gain the whole world, yet forfeit their soul?
~Mark 8:36

DID I PRAY?

YES   NO

DID I SPEND TIME WITH GOD?

YES   NO

WHAT AM I GRATEFUL FOR TODAY?

WHAT DID I FEED MY SOUL?

BOOKS	PODCASTS	VERSES

DID I WIN THE BATTLE OF THE MIND?
~2 Cor 10:3-5

CHOOSE A VERSE THAT RESONATAES WITH YOU.
HOW DOES THIS VERSE APPLY TO YOUR LIFE?

MIND

"I the Lord search the heart and examine the mind, to reward each person according to their conduct, according to what their deeds deserve."
~Jer 17:10

HOW DO YOU FEEL?

HOW DID YOU INVEST IN YOURSELF?

BODY

Your eye is the lamp of your body. When your eyes are healthy, your whole body also is full of light. But when they are unhealthy, your body also is full of darkness.
~Luke 11:34

BREAKFAST

SLEEP

QUALITY   TOTAL HOURS

LUNCH

MOOD   WATER

DID I TAKE MY VITAMINS?

WEATHER

YES [ ]   NO [ ]

SNACKS

EXERCISE

TYPE

TIME

TOTAL STEPS

DINNER

SOUL

What good is it for someone to gain the whole world, yet forfeit their soul?
~Mark 8:36

DID I PRAY?

YES   NO

DID I SPEND TIME WITH GOD?

YES   NO

WHAT AM I GRATEFUL FOR TODAY?

WHAT DID I FEED MY SOUL?

BOOKS

PODCASTS

VERSES

DID I WIN THE BATTLE OF THE MIND?
~2 Cor 10:3-5

CHOOSE A VERSE THAT RESONATAES WITH YOU.
HOW DOES THIS VERSE APPLY TO YOUR LIFE?

MIND

"I the Lord search the heart and examine the mind, to reward each person
according to their conduct, according to what their deeds deserve."
~Jer 17:10

HOW DO YOU FEEL?

HOW DID YOU INVEST IN YOURSELF?

BODY

Your eye is the lamp of your body. When your eyes are healthy, your whole body also is full of light. But when they are unhealthy, your body also is full of darkness.
~Luke 11:34

BREAKFAST

SLEEP

QUALITY

TOTAL HOURS

LUNCH

MOOD

WATER

DID I TAKE MY VITAMINS?

YES ☐ NO ☐

WEATHER

SNACKS

EXERCISE

TYPE

TIME

TOTAL STEPS

DINNER

SOUL

What good is it for someone to gain the whole world, yet forfeit their soul?
~Mark 8:36

DID I PRAY?

YES   NO

DID I SPEND TIME WITH GOD?

YES   NO

WHAT AM I GRATEFUL FOR TODAY?

WHAT DID I FEED MY SOUL?

BOOKS	PODCASTS	VERSES

DID I WIN THE BATTLE OF THE MIND?
~2 Cor 10:3-5

**CHOOSE A VERSE THAT RESONATAES WITH YOU.
HOW DOES THIS VERSE APPLY TO YOUR LIFE?**

MIND

DATE

"I the Lord search the heart and examine the mind, to reward each person according to their conduct, according to what their deeds deserve."
~Jer 17:10

HOW DO YOU FEEL?

HOW DID YOU INVEST IN YOURSELF?

BODY

Your eye is the lamp of your body. When your eyes are healthy, your whole body also is full of light. But when they are unhealthy, your body also is full of darkness.
~Luke 11:34

BREAKFAST

SLEEP

QUALITY

TOTAL HOURS

LUNCH

MOOD

WATER

DID I TAKE MY VITAMINS?

YES ▢   NO ▢

WEATHER

SNACKS

EXERCISE

TYPE

TIME

TOTAL STEPS

DINNER

SOUL

What good is it for someone to gain the whole world, yet forfeit their soul?
~Mark 8:36

DID I PRAY?

YES   NO

DID I SPEND TIME WITH GOD?

YES   NO

WHAT AM I GRATEFUL FOR TODAY?

WHAT DID I FEED MY SOUL?

BOOKS

PODCASTS

VERSES

DID I WIN THE BATTLE OF THE MIND?
~2 Cor 10:3-5

**CHOOSE A VERSE THAT RESONATAES WITH YOU.
HOW DOES THIS VERSE APPLY TO YOUR LIFE?**

MIND

"I the Lord search the heart and examine the mind, to reward each person according to their conduct, according to what their deeds deserve."
~Jer 17:10

HOW DO YOU FEEL?

HOW DID YOU INVEST IN YOURSELF?

BODY

Your eye is the lamp of your body. When your eyes are healthy, your whole body also is full of light. But when they are unhealthy, your body also is full of darkness.
~Luke 11:34

BREAKFAST

SLEEP

QUALITY

TOTAL HOURS

LUNCH

MOOD

WATER

DID I TAKE MY VITAMINS?

YES ▢   NO ▢

WEATHER

SNACKS

EXERCISE

TYPE

TIME

TOTAL STEPS

DINNER

SOUL

What good is it for someone to gain the whole world, yet forfeit their soul?
~Mark 8:36

DID I PRAY?

YES   NO

DID I SPEND TIME WITH GOD?

YES   NO

WHAT AM I GRATEFUL FOR TODAY?

WHAT DID I FEED MY SOUL?

BOOKS

PODCASTS

VERSES

DID I WIN THE BATTLE OF THE MIND?
~2 Cor 10:3-5

CHOOSE A VERSE THAT RESONATAES WITH YOU.
HOW DOES THIS VERSE APPLY TO YOUR LIFE?

MIND

"I the Lord search the heart and examine the mind, to reward each person according to their conduct, according to what their deeds deserve."
~Jer 17:10

HOW DO YOU FEEL?

HOW DID YOU INVEST IN YOURSELF?

BODY

Your eye is the lamp of your body. When your eyes are healthy, your whole body also is full of light. But when they are unhealthy, your body also is full of darkness.
~Luke 11:34

BREAKFAST

SLEEP

QUALITY   **TOTAL HOURS**

LUNCH

MOOD   **WATER**

DID I TAKE MY VITAMINS?

YES ☐   NO ☐

WEATHER

SNACKS

EXERCISE

TYPE

TIME

TOTAL STEPS

DINNER

SOUL

What good is it for someone to gain the whole world, yet forfeit their soul?
~Mark 8:36

DID I PRAY?

YES ☐   NO ☐

DID I SPEND TIME WITH GOD?

YES ☐   NO ☐

WHAT AM I GRATEFUL FOR TODAY?

WHAT DID I FEED MY SOUL?

BOOKS	PODCASTS	VERSES

DID I WIN THE BATTLE OF THE MIND?
~2 Cor 10:3-5

CHOOSE A VERSE THAT RESONATAES WITH YOU.
HOW DOES THIS VERSE APPLY TO YOUR LIFE?

MIND

"I the Lord search the heart and examine the mind, to reward each person according to their conduct, according to what their deeds deserve."
~Jer 17:10

HOW DO YOU FEEL?

HOW DID YOU INVEST IN YOURSELF?

BODY

Your eye is the lamp of your body. When your eyes are healthy, your whole body also is full of light. But when they are unhealthy, your body also is full of darkness.
~Luke 11:34

BREAKFAST

SLEEP

QUALITY

TOTAL HOURS

LUNCH

MOOD

WATER

DID I TAKE MY VITAMINS?

YES ☐   NO ☐

WEATHER

SNACKS

EXERCISE

TYPE

TIME

TOTAL STEPS

DINNER

SOUL

What good is it for someone to gain the whole world, yet forfeit their soul?
~Mark 8:36

DID I PRAY?

YES ☐　　NO ☐

DID I SPEND TIME WITH GOD?

YES ☐　　NO ☐

WHAT AM I GRATEFUL FOR TODAY?

WHAT DID I FEED MY SOUL?

BOOKS	PODCASTS	VERSES

DID I WIN THE BATTLE OF THE MIND?
~2 Cor 10:3-5

CHOOSE A VERSE THAT RESONATAES WITH YOU.
HOW DOES THIS VERSE APPLY TO YOUR LIFE?

MIND

"I the Lord search the heart and examine the mind, to reward each person according to their conduct, according to what their deeds deserve."
~Jer 17:10

HOW DO YOU FEEL?

HOW DID YOU INVEST IN YOURSELF?

BODY

Your eye is the lamp of your body. When your eyes are healthy, your whole body also is full of light. But when they are unhealthy, your body also is full of darkness.
~Luke 11:34

BREAKFAST

SLEEP

QUALITY

TOTAL HOURS

LUNCH

MOOD

WATER

DID I TAKE MY VITAMINS?

YES ☐ NO ☐

WEATHER

SNACKS

EXERCISE

TYPE

TIME

TOTAL STEPS

DINNER

SOUL

What good is it for someone to gain the whole world, yet forfeit their soul?
~Mark 8:36

DID I PRAY?

YES ☐   NO ☐

DID I SPEND TIME WITH GOD?

YES ☐   NO ☐

WHAT AM I GRATEFUL FOR TODAY?

WHAT DID I FEED MY SOUL?

BOOKS

PODCASTS

VERSES

DID I WIN THE BATTLE OF THE MIND?
~2 Cor 10:3-5

CHOOSE A VERSE THAT RESONATAES WITH YOU.
HOW DOES THIS VERSE APPLY TO YOUR LIFE?

MIND

"I the Lord search the heart and examine the mind, to reward each person according to their conduct, according to what their deeds deserve."
~Jer 17:10

HOW DO YOU FEEL?

HOW DID YOU INVEST IN YOURSELF?

BODY

Your eye is the lamp of your body. When your eyes are healthy, your whole body also is full of light. But when they are unhealthy, your body also is full of darkness.
~Luke 11:34

BREAKFAST

SLEEP

QUALITY

TOTAL HOURS

LUNCH

MOOD

WATER

DID I TAKE MY VITAMINS?

YES ☐   NO ☐

WEATHER

SNACKS

EXERCISE

TYPE

TIME

TOTAL STEPS

DINNER

SOUL

What good is it for someone to gain the whole world, yet forfeit their soul?
~Mark 8:36

DID I PRAY?

YES   NO

DID I SPEND TIME WITH GOD?

YES   NO

WHAT AM I GRATEFUL FOR TODAY?

WHAT DID I FEED MY SOUL?

BOOKS	PODCASTS	VERSES

DID I WIN THE BATTLE OF THE MIND?

~2 Cor 10:3-5

CHOOSE A VERSE THAT RESONATAES WITH YOU.
HOW DOES THIS VERSE APPLY TO YOUR LIFE?

MIND

"I the Lord search the heart and examine the mind, to reward each person according to their conduct, according to what their deeds deserve."
~Jer 17:10

HOW DO YOU FEEL?

HOW DID YOU INVEST IN YOURSELF?

BODY

Your eye is the lamp of your body. When your eyes are healthy, your whole body also is full of light. But when they are unhealthy, your body also is full of darkness.
~Luke 11:34

BREAKFAST

SLEEP

QUALITY   **TOTAL HOURS**

LUNCH

MOOD   **WATER**

DID I TAKE MY VITAMINS?

YES ☐   NO ☐

WEATHER

SNACKS

EXERCISE

TYPE

TIME

TOTAL STEPS

DINNER

SOUL

What good is it for someone to gain the whole world, yet forfeit their soul?
~Mark 8:36

DID I PRAY?

YES   NO

DID I SPEND TIME WITH GOD?

YES   NO

WHAT AM I GRATEFUL FOR TODAY?

WHAT DID I FEED MY SOUL?

BOOKS

PODCASTS

VERSES

DID I WIN THE BATTLE OF THE MIND?
~2 Cor 10:3-5

CHOOSE A VERSE THAT RESONATAES WITH YOU.
HOW DOES THIS VERSE APPLY TO YOUR LIFE?

MIND

"I the Lord search the heart and examine the mind, to reward each person according to their conduct, according to what their deeds deserve."
~Jer 17:10

HOW DO YOU FEEL?

HOW DID YOU INVEST IN YOURSELF?

BODY

Your eye is the lamp of your body. When your eyes are healthy, your whole body also is full of light. But when they are unhealthy, your body also is full of darkness.
~Luke 11:34

BREAKFAST

SLEEP

QUALITY

TOTAL HOURS

LUNCH

MOOD

WATER

DID I TAKE MY VITAMINS?

YES ☐   NO ☐

WEATHER

SNACKS

EXERCISE

TYPE

TIME

TOTAL STEPS

DINNER

SOUL

What good is it for someone to gain the whole world, yet forfeit their soul?
~Mark 8:36

DID I PRAY?

YES ☐   NO ☐

DID I SPEND TIME WITH GOD?

YES ☐   NO ☐

WHAT AM I GRATEFUL FOR TODAY?

WHAT DID I FEED MY SOUL?

BOOKS	PODCASTS	VERSES

DID I WIN THE BATTLE OF THE MIND?
~2 Cor 10:3-5

CHOOSE A VERSE THAT RESONATAES WITH YOU.
HOW DOES THIS VERSE APPLY TO YOUR LIFE?

MIND

"I the Lord search the heart and examine the mind, to reward each person according to their conduct, according to what their deeds deserve."
~Jer 17:10

HOW DO YOU FEEL?

HOW DID YOU INVEST IN YOURSELF?

BODY

Your eye is the lamp of your body. When your eyes are healthy, your whole body also is full of light. But when they are unhealthy, your body also is full of darkness.
~Luke 11:34

BREAKFAST

SLEEP

QUALITY

TOTAL HOURS

LUNCH

MOOD

WATER

DID I TAKE MY VITAMINS?

YES ▢ NO ▢

WEATHER

SNACKS

EXERCISE

TYPE

TIME

TOTAL STEPS

DINNER

SOUL

What good is it for someone to gain the whole world, yet forfeit their soul?
~Mark 8:36

DID I PRAY?

YES ☐   NO ☐

DID I SPEND TIME WITH GOD?

YES ☐   NO ☐

WHAT AM I GRATEFUL FOR TODAY?

WHAT DID I FEED MY SOUL?

BOOKS

PODCASTS

VERSES

DID I WIN THE BATTLE OF THE MIND?
~2 Cor 10:3-5

**CHOOSE A VERSE THAT RESONATAES WITH YOU.
HOW DOES THIS VERSE APPLY TO YOUR LIFE?**

MIND

"I the Lord search the heart and examine the mind, to reward each person according to their conduct, according to what their deeds deserve."
~Jer 17:10

HOW DO YOU FEEL?

HOW DID YOU INVEST IN YOURSELF?

BODY

Your eye is the lamp of your body. When your eyes are healthy, your whole body also is full of light. But when they are unhealthy, your body also is full of darkness.
~Luke 11:34

BREAKFAST

SLEEP

QUALITY

TOTAL HOURS

LUNCH

MOOD

WATER

DID I TAKE MY VITAMINS?

YES

NO

WEATHER

SNACKS

EXERCISE

TYPE

TIME

TOTAL STEPS

DINNER

SOUL

What good is it for someone to gain the whole world, yet forfeit their soul?
~Mark 8:36

DID I PRAY?

YES ☐   NO ☐

DID I SPEND TIME WITH GOD?

YES ☐   NO ☐

WHAT AM I GRATEFUL FOR TODAY?

WHAT DID I FEED MY SOUL?

BOOKS	PODCASTS	VERSES

DID I WIN THE BATTLE OF THE MIND?
~2 Cor 10:3-5

CHOOSE A VERSE THAT RESONATAES WITH YOU.
HOW DOES THIS VERSE APPLY TO YOUR LIFE?

MIND

"I the Lord search the heart and examine the mind, to reward each person according to their conduct, according to what their deeds deserve."
~Jer 17:10

HOW DO YOU FEEL?

HOW DID YOU INVEST IN YOURSELF?

BODY

Your eye is the lamp of your body. When your eyes are healthy, your whole body also is full of light. But when they are unhealthy, your body also is full of darkness.
~Luke 11:34

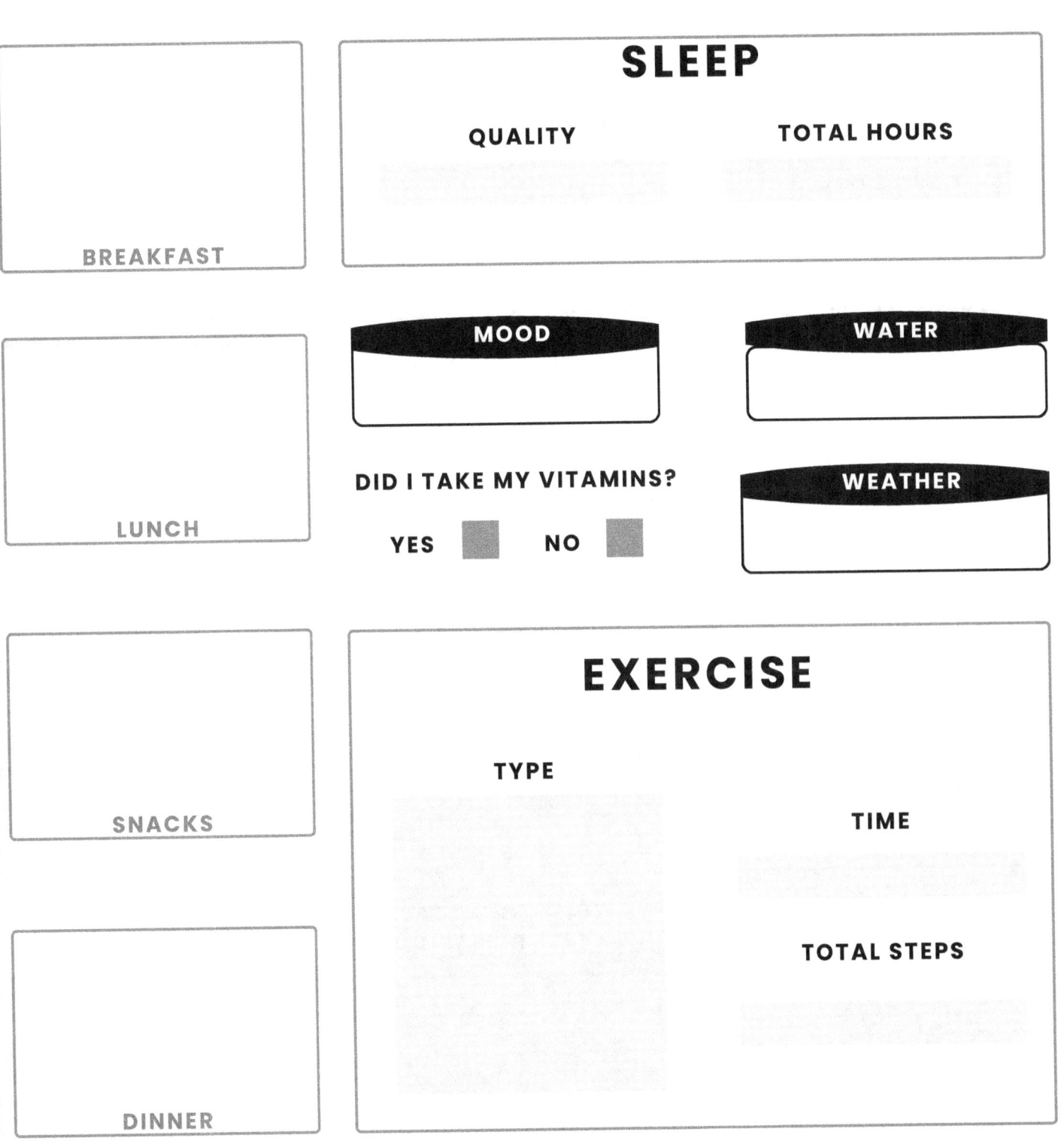

BREAKFAST

SLEEP

QUALITY

TOTAL HOURS

LUNCH

MOOD

WATER

DID I TAKE MY VITAMINS?

YES   NO

WEATHER

SNACKS

EXERCISE

TYPE

TIME

TOTAL STEPS

DINNER

SOUL

What good is it for someone to gain the whole world, yet forfeit their soul?
~Mark 8:36

DID I PRAY?

YES   NO

DID I SPEND TIME WITH GOD?

YES   NO

WHAT AM I GRATEFUL FOR TODAY?

WHAT DID I FEED MY SOUL?

BOOKS	PODCASTS	VERSES

DID I WIN THE BATTLE OF THE MIND?
~2 Cor 10:3-5

CHOOSE A VERSE THAT RESONATAES WITH YOU. HOW DOES THIS VERSE APPLY TO YOUR LIFE?

MIND

"I the Lord search the heart and examine the mind, to reward each person according to their conduct, according to what their deeds deserve."
~Jer 17:10

HOW DO YOU FEEL?

HOW DID YOU INVEST IN YOURSELF?

BODY

Your eye is the lamp of your body. When your eyes are healthy, your whole body also is full of light. But when they are unhealthy, your body also is full of darkness.
~Luke 11:34

BREAKFAST

SLEEP

QUALITY   TOTAL HOURS

LUNCH

MOOD   WATER

DID I TAKE MY VITAMINS?   WEATHER

YES   NO

SNACKS

EXERCISE

TYPE

TIME

TOTAL STEPS

DINNER

SOUL

What good is it for someone to gain the whole world, yet forfeit their soul?
~Mark 8:36

DID I PRAY?

YES   NO

DID I SPEND TIME WITH GOD?

YES   NO

WHAT AM I GRATEFUL FOR TODAY?

WHAT DID I FEED MY SOUL?

BOOKS

PODCASTS

VERSES

DID I WIN THE BATTLE OF THE MIND?
~2 Cor 10:3-5

CHOOSE A VERSE THAT RESONATAES WITH YOU.
HOW DOES THIS VERSE APPLY TO YOUR LIFE?

MIND

"I the Lord search the heart and examine the mind, to reward each person according to their conduct, according to what their deeds deserve."
~Jer 17:10

HOW DO YOU FEEL?

HOW DID YOU INVEST IN YOURSELF?

BODY

Your eye is the lamp of your body. When your eyes are healthy, your whole body also is full of light. But when they are unhealthy, your body also is full of darkness.
~Luke 11:34

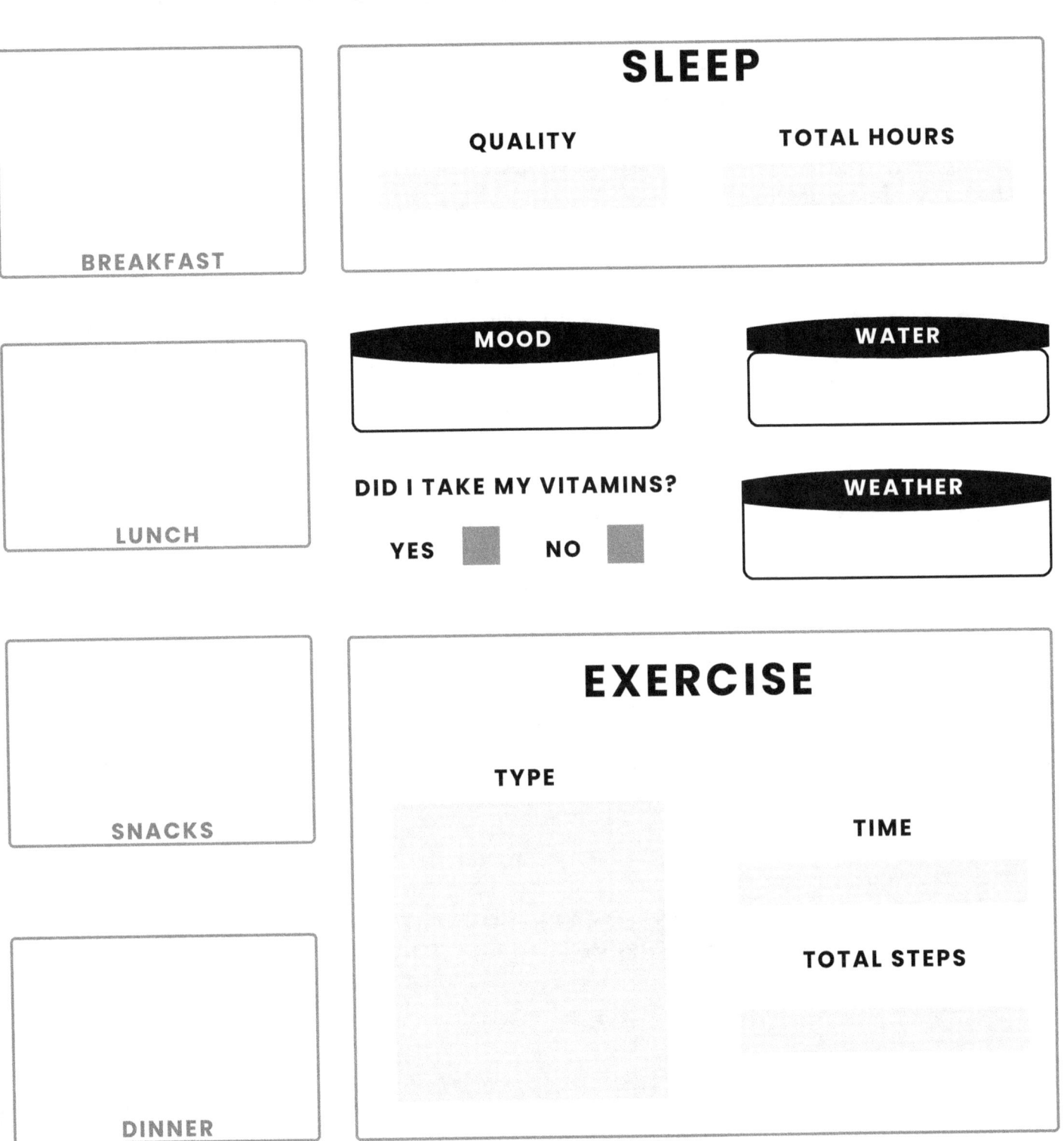

BREAKFAST

SLEEP

QUALITY

TOTAL HOURS

LUNCH

MOOD

WATER

DID I TAKE MY VITAMINS?

YES   NO

WEATHER

SNACKS

EXERCISE

TYPE

TIME

TOTAL STEPS

DINNER

SOUL

What good is it for someone to gain the whole world, yet forfeit their soul?
~Mark 8:36

DID I PRAY?

YES   NO

DID I SPEND TIME WITH GOD?

YES   NO

WHAT AM I GRATEFUL FOR TODAY?

WHAT DID I FEED MY SOUL?

BOOKS

PODCASTS

VERSES

DID I WIN THE BATTLE OF THE MIND?
~2 Cor 10:3-5

**CHOOSE A VERSE THAT RESONATAES WITH YOU.
HOW DOES THIS VERSE APPLY TO YOUR LIFE?**

MIND

"I the Lord search the heart and examine the mind, to reward each person according to their conduct, according to what their deeds deserve."
~Jer 17:10

HOW DO YOU FEEL?

HOW DID YOU INVEST IN YOURSELF?

BODY

Your eye is the lamp of your body. When your eyes are healthy, your whole body also is full of light. But when they are unhealthy, your body also is full of darkness.
~Luke 11:34

BREAKFAST

SLEEP

QUALITY

TOTAL HOURS

LUNCH

MOOD

WATER

DID I TAKE MY VITAMINS?

YES ☐ NO ☐

WEATHER

SNACKS

EXERCISE

TYPE

TIME

TOTAL STEPS

DINNER

SOUL

What good is it for someone to gain the whole world, yet forfeit their soul?
~Mark 8:36

DID I PRAY?

YES   NO

DID I SPEND TIME WITH GOD?

YES   NO

WHAT AM I GRATEFUL FOR TODAY?

WHAT DID I FEED MY SOUL?

BOOKS	PODCASTS	VERSES

DID I WIN THE BATTLE OF THE MIND?
~2 Cor 10:3-5

CHOOSE A VERSE THAT RESONATAES WITH YOU.
HOW DOES THIS VERSE APPLY TO YOUR LIFE?

MIND

"I the Lord search the heart and examine the mind, to reward each person according to their conduct, according to what their deeds deserve."
~Jer 17:10

HOW DO YOU FEEL?

HOW DID YOU INVEST IN YOURSELF?

BODY

Your eye is the lamp of your body. When your eyes are healthy, your whole body also is full of light. But when they are unhealthy, your body also is full of darkness.
~Luke 11:34

BREAKFAST

SLEEP

QUALITY

TOTAL HOURS

LUNCH

MOOD

WATER

DID I TAKE MY VITAMINS?

YES ☐ NO ☐

WEATHER

SNACKS

EXERCISE

TYPE

TIME

TOTAL STEPS

DINNER

SOUL

What good is it for someone to gain the whole world, yet forfeit their soul?
~Mark 8:36

DID I PRAY?

YES ☐   NO ☐

DID I SPEND TIME WITH GOD?

YES ☐   NO ☐

WHAT AM I GRATEFUL FOR TODAY?

WHAT DID I FEED MY SOUL?

BOOKS

PODCASTS

VERSES

DID I WIN THE BATTLE OF THE MIND?

~2 Cor 10:3-5

CHOOSE A VERSE THAT RESONATAES WITH YOU.
HOW DOES THIS VERSE APPLY TO YOUR LIFE?

MIND

"I the Lord search the heart and examine the mind, to reward each person according to their conduct, according to what their deeds deserve."
~Jer 17:10

HOW DO YOU FEEL?

HOW DID YOU INVEST IN YOURSELF?

BODY

Your eye is the lamp of your body. When your eyes are healthy, your whole body also is full of light. But when they are unhealthy, your body also is full of darkness.
~Luke 11:34

BREAKFAST

SLEEP

QUALITY   TOTAL HOURS

LUNCH

MOOD   WATER

DID I TAKE MY VITAMINS?   WEATHER

YES [ ]   NO [ ]

SNACKS

EXERCISE

TYPE

TIME

TOTAL STEPS

DINNER

SOUL

What good is it for someone to gain the whole world, yet forfeit their soul?
~Mark 8:36

DID I PRAY?

YES   NO

DID I SPEND TIME WITH GOD?

YES   NO

WHAT AM I GRATEFUL FOR TODAY?

WHAT DID I FEED MY SOUL?

BOOKS

PODCASTS

VERSES

DID I WIN THE BATTLE OF THE MIND?
~2 Cor 10:3-5

CHOOSE A VERSE THAT RESONATAES WITH YOU.
HOW DOES THIS VERSE APPLY TO YOUR LIFE?

MIND

"I the Lord search the heart and examine the mind, to reward each person according to their conduct, according to what their deeds deserve."
~Jer 17:10

HOW DO YOU FEEL?

HOW DID YOU INVEST IN YOURSELF?

BODY

Your eye is the lamp of your body. When your eyes are healthy, your whole body also is full of light. But when they are unhealthy, your body also is full of darkness.
~Luke 11:34

BREAKFAST

SLEEP

QUALITY

TOTAL HOURS

LUNCH

MOOD

WATER

DID I TAKE MY VITAMINS?

YES   NO

WEATHER

SNACKS

EXERCISE

TYPE

TIME

TOTAL STEPS

DINNER

SOUL

What good is it for someone to gain the whole world, yet forfeit their soul?
~Mark 8:36

DID I PRAY?

YES   NO

DID I SPEND TIME WITH GOD?

YES   NO

WHAT AM I GRATEFUL FOR TODAY?

WHAT DID I FEED MY SOUL?

BOOKS	PODCASTS	VERSES

DID I WIN THE BATTLE OF THE MIND?
~2 Cor 10:3-5

**CHOOSE A VERSE THAT RESONATAES WITH YOU.
HOW DOES THIS VERSE APPLY TO YOUR LIFE?**

MIND

"I the Lord search the heart and examine the mind, to reward each person according to their conduct, according to what their deeds deserve."
~Jer 17:10

HOW DO YOU FEEL?

HOW DID YOU INVEST IN YOURSELF?

BODY

Your eye is the lamp of your body. When your eyes are healthy, your whole body also is full of light. But when they are unhealthy, your body also is full of darkness.
~Luke 11:34

BREAKFAST

SLEEP

QUALITY

TOTAL HOURS

LUNCH

MOOD

WATER

DID I TAKE MY VITAMINS?

YES [ ]   NO [ ]

WEATHER

SNACKS

EXERCISE

TYPE

TIME

TOTAL STEPS

DINNER

SOUL

What good is it for someone to gain the whole world, yet forfeit their soul?
~Mark 8:36

DID I PRAY?

YES ☐   NO ☐

DID I SPEND TIME WITH GOD?

YES ☐   NO ☐

WHAT AM I GRATEFUL FOR TODAY?

WHAT DID I FEED MY SOUL?

BOOKS	PODCASTS	VERSES

DID I WIN THE BATTLE OF THE MIND?
~2 Cor 10:3-5

CHOOSE A VERSE THAT RESONATAES WITH YOU.
HOW DOES THIS VERSE APPLY TO YOUR LIFE?

MIND

DATE

"I the Lord search the heart and examine the mind, to reward each person according to their conduct, according to what their deeds deserve."
~Jer 17:10

HOW DO YOU FEEL?

HOW DID YOU INVEST IN YOURSELF?

BODY

Your eye is the lamp of your body. When your eyes are healthy, your whole body also is full of light. But when they are unhealthy, your body also is full of darkness.
~Luke 11:34

BREAKFAST

SLEEP

QUALITY

TOTAL HOURS

LUNCH

MOOD

WATER

DID I TAKE MY VITAMINS?

YES ☐ NO ☐

WEATHER

SNACKS

EXERCISE

TYPE

TIME

TOTAL STEPS

DINNER

SOUL

What good is it for someone to gain the whole world, yet forfeit their soul?
~Mark 8:36

DID I PRAY?

YES ☐   NO ☐

DID I SPEND TIME WITH GOD?

YES ☐   NO ☐

WHAT AM I GRATEFUL FOR TODAY?

WHAT DID I FEED MY SOUL?

BOOKS

PODCASTS

VERSES

DID I WIN THE BATTLE OF THE MIND?
~2 Cor 10:3-5

CHOOSE A VERSE THAT RESONATAES WITH YOU.
HOW DOES THIS VERSE APPLY TO YOUR LIFE?

MIND

"I the Lord search the heart and examine the mind, to reward each person according to their conduct, according to what their deeds deserve."
~Jer 17:10

HOW DO YOU FEEL?

HOW DID YOU INVEST IN YOURSELF?

BODY

Your eye is the lamp of your body. When your eyes are healthy, your whole body also is full of light. But when they are unhealthy, your body also is full of darkness.
~Luke 11:34

BREAKFAST

SLEEP

QUALITY   TOTAL HOURS

LUNCH

MOOD

WATER

DID I TAKE MY VITAMINS?

YES   NO

WEATHER

SNACKS

EXERCISE

TYPE

TIME

TOTAL STEPS

DINNER

SOUL

What good is it for someone to gain the whole world, yet forfeit their soul?
~Mark 8:36

DID I PRAY?

YES ☐   NO ☐

DID I SPEND TIME WITH GOD?

YES ☐   NO ☐

WHAT AM I GRATEFUL FOR TODAY?

WHAT DID I FEED MY SOUL?

BOOKS	PODCASTS	VERSES

DID I WIN THE BATTLE OF THE MIND?
~2 Cor 10:3-5

CHOOSE A VERSE THAT RESONATAES WITH YOU.
HOW DOES THIS VERSE APPLY TO YOUR LIFE?

MIND

"I the Lord search the heart and examine the mind, to reward each person according to their conduct, according to what their deeds deserve."
~Jer 17:10

HOW DO YOU FEEL?

HOW DID YOU INVEST IN YOURSELF?

BODY

Your eye is the lamp of your body. When your eyes are healthy, your whole body also is full of light. But when they are unhealthy, your body also is full of darkness.
~Luke 11:34

BREAKFAST

SLEEP

QUALITY   TOTAL HOURS

LUNCH

MOOD   WATER

DID I TAKE MY VITAMINS?

YES ☐   NO ☐

WEATHER

SNACKS

EXERCISE

TYPE

TIME

TOTAL STEPS

DINNER

SOUL

What good is it for someone to gain the whole world, yet forfeit their soul?
~Mark 8:36

DID I PRAY?

YES ☐   NO ☐

DID I SPEND TIME WITH GOD?

YES ☐   NO ☐

WHAT AM I GRATEFUL FOR TODAY?

WHAT DID I FEED MY SOUL?

BOOKS	PODCASTS	VERSES

DID I WIN THE BATTLE OF THE MIND?
~2 Cor 10:3-5

CHOOSE A VERSE THAT RESONATAES WITH YOU.
HOW DOES THIS VERSE APPLY TO YOUR LIFE?

MIND

"I the Lord search the heart and examine the mind, to reward each person according to their conduct, according to what their deeds deserve."
~Jer 17:10

HOW DO YOU FEEL?

HOW DID YOU INVEST IN YOURSELF?

BODY

Your eye is the lamp of your body. When your eyes are healthy, your whole body also is full of light. But when they are unhealthy, your body also is full of darkness.
~Luke 11:34

BREAKFAST

SLEEP

QUALITY

TOTAL HOURS

LUNCH

MOOD

WATER

DID I TAKE MY VITAMINS?

YES ☐   NO ☐

WEATHER

SNACKS

EXERCISE

TYPE

TIME

TOTAL STEPS

DINNER

SOUL

What good is it for someone to gain the whole world, yet forfeit their soul?
~Mark 8:36

DID I PRAY?

YES ☐   NO ☐

DID I SPEND TIME WITH GOD?

YES ☐   NO ☐

WHAT AM I GRATEFUL FOR TODAY?

WHAT DID I FEED MY SOUL?

BOOKS

PODCASTS

VERSES

DID I WIN THE BATTLE OF THE MIND?
~2 Cor 10:3-5

CHOOSE A VERSE THAT RESONATAES WITH YOU.
HOW DOES THIS VERSE APPLY TO YOUR LIFE?

MIND

"I the Lord search the heart and examine the mind, to reward each person according to their conduct, according to what their deeds deserve."
~Jer 17:10

HOW DO YOU FEEL?

HOW DID YOU INVEST IN YOURSELF?

BODY

Your eye is the lamp of your body. When your eyes are healthy, your whole body also is full of light. But when they are unhealthy, your body also is full of darkness.
~Luke 11:34

BREAKFAST

SLEEP

QUALITY

TOTAL HOURS

LUNCH

MOOD

WATER

DID I TAKE MY VITAMINS?

YES   NO

WEATHER

SNACKS

EXERCISE

TYPE

TIME

TOTAL STEPS

DINNER

SOUL

What good is it for someone to gain the whole world, yet forfeit their soul?
~Mark 8:36

DID I PRAY?

YES   NO

DID I SPEND TIME WITH GOD?

YES   NO

WHAT AM I GRATEFUL FOR TODAY?

WHAT DID I FEED MY SOUL?

BOOKS

PODCASTS

VERSES

DID I WIN THE BATTLE OF THE MIND?
~2 Cor 10:3-5

CHOOSE A VERSE THAT RESONATAES WITH YOU.
HOW DOES THIS VERSE APPLY TO YOUR LIFE?

How can my life be
Extraordinary?

Being single doesn't mean that your life is on hold. Viewing your life from this perspective will cause you to miss out on opportunities, growth, and joy. By answering these thoughtful questions, you'll understand what embracing independence means and rediscovering your passions. This isn't about what's missing; it's about seeing all that's already within you. With each answer, you'll uncover new ways to nurture your well-being, cultivate meaningful relationships, and design an extraordinary life—just as you are right now.

Living happily ever after isn't reserved for couples or fairy tales; it's about writing your own story. The questions ahead will guide you to reflect on your dreams, identify what brings you joy, and break free from limiting beliefs about what it means to be single. You'll learn how to celebrate your journey and build a life so rich with meaning and purpose that it naturally draws the right opportunities—and people—into your path. Sis, I want you to take a deep breath, lean in, and let this be the beginning of your happily ever after.

Chapter 1

Are you single?

What does living an extraordinary life look like to you?

Do you want to get married?

What is your idea of a successful marriage?

Do you want children?

Are you single by choice?

How do you view being single?

Do you enjoy being single?

Why do you believe so many beautiful, kind, intelligent, talented Christian women are walking around discontent, sad, tired, or complaining about being "stuck" on Single Avenue?

How do you feel when people inquire about your marital status?

Do you believe that your happiness is contingent on your marital status?

Do you feel less than enough?

Describe your garden.

Describe a pristine garden vs. a hot mess garden.

What steps will you take to clean up your garden?

What God-given gifts do you believe God has entrusted to you?

Do you view yourself as a damsel in distress?

Are you intentional with how you spend your time?

What healthy habits do you want to establish?

How do you align your mind, body, and soul?

Why does Apostle Paul believe it is better to remain single?

What does it mean to be a fully converted Christian?

Are you a fully converted Christian?

What kind of "fruit" are you producing in your life?

Why did Christ curse the fig tree?

What does it mean to have a checklist lifestyle?

What are the dangers of living a checklist lifestyle?

Name the differences between #TeamItsAllGood vs. #TeamKeepItReal.

What are the dangers of listening to information from #Teamitsallgood?

True or False: Whether marriage and children are in the cards for you, you can still have the happily ever after ending you desire. Do you agree or disagree?

How do you handle detours?

How have you let Jesus control your life?

Chapter 2

Are there weeds in your garden?

What fiery darts has Satan thrown at you?

Name the "trees" that God has blessed you with the opportunity to enjoy that you have taken for granted.

Explain Matt. 7:6 and how it applies to your life.

Name all the characteristics that the woman in Psalm 31 possesses.

What is keeping you from having a pristine garden?

What is holding you back from being all in with God?

Do you doubt that God will provide for you? If so, why?

Has God ever failed to provide for you?

Do you believe that God can do the impossible?

If you continue to doubt God, do you believe your decision to purposely remain in doubt will result in regret?

What weeds do you need to remove from your garden?

How will you plant more seeds (aka God's word)?

Do you believe you're subscribed to God's trial and tribulation package or the soft life package?

When faced with adversity, what do you do? What should you do?

True or False: Singlehood is a problem.

How can fear be a blessing and a curse?

Name the weeds that attempt to enter your mental filter.

Weed:

Capture:

Examine:

Destroy or Embrace:

Weed:

Capture:

Examine:

Destroy or Embrace:

Weed:

Capture:

Examine:

Destroy or Embrace:

Weed:

Capture:

Examine:

Destroy or Embrace:

Weed:

Capture:

Examine:

Destroy or Embrace:

Weed:

Capture:

Examine:

Destroy or Embrace:

Are you careful with what you consume?

What are your criteria for content that is pure and honest?

Why do people consider the Bible as a giant to-do list?

God promises us a peace that surpasses all understanding. Why are many single Christian women not experiencing this peace? John 16:33 Do you have peace? If not, why do you believe you do not have peace?

Chapter 3

Have you prayed for a husband?

True or False: Praying for a husband is a colossal waste of time.

What are your thoughts regarding Christian dating coaches?

What will your dash look like?

How will you close the door to fear?

What spiritual words are you speaking over your life? List your favorite verses.

How will you close the door to fear?

How do you fill your soul with God's word?

How will you let God direct your steps daily?

How will you cultivate your God-given gifts?

How can you help others discover and cultivate their gifts while God leads you to your destiny?

What does a healthy boundary look like?

Think of an example where you did not set a healthy boundary. How did you feel?

How will you enforce healthy boundaries in your life?

Chapter 4

Do you believe that you are broken or incomplete due to your single marital status?

How can we use the Bible as medication to help us get well?

How should you approach unsolicited advice about your life?

Proverbs 18:22 says, " A man that finds a wife finds a good thing and obtains favor from the Lord." How does this verse make you feel?

Regardless of whether you desire to be "found," how will you work on yourself?

How do you get to know someone you are interested in dating?

How have you developed a relationship with God?

Name the pieces of spiritual armor we need to wear to defeat Satan.

What armor piece (s) do you need to be more intentional in wearing to protect yourself? What happens when you fail to wear that piece(s) of armor?

Name the external and internal attributes that we need to possess.

What attributes do you possess?

What attributes do you need to gain?

What is the difference between external and internal attributes?

How are the attributes similar to an onion?

What layers of your onion are you missing?

Chapter 5

Write a description for each one of the below External Attributes.

Love

Joy

Peace

Patience

Kindness

What lessons can we learn from the Good Samaritan?

How can we show kindness?

How can Haggai 1: 5-7 apply to your finances?

Chapter 6

Describe each of the below internal attributes.

Faithfulness

Self-control

Forgiving

Wisdom

Courage

Forgiveness does not mean access. What does this mean to you?

Name someone in your life who has courage. How do they display courage?

Why do women confuse sex with love?

How has God disciplined you? What lessons did you learn?

Describe your emotions during each of these seasons of your life.

SPRING

SUMMER

FALL

Winter

Are there triggers that cause you to feel this way? What lessons did you learn during each of these seasons?

What season best describes your life right now?

What brings you joy?

How can you find joy in a challenging situation?

How can you bring joy to others?

Why should our emotions not dictate our outlook on life?

How can you feel the peace that surpasses understanding?

Read James 1:8. What does it mean to be double-minded?

Are you double-minded?

How can you avoid being double-minded?

When you revisit your past, what lessons have you learned?

What is the difference between a bad hand and a good hand?

What are the good hands in your life?

What are the bad hands in your life?

How have you played those cards (how have you reacted)?

Name the ways we can incorporate peace into our lives. Why is it difficult to be patient?

What causes you to feel impatient?

Name some consequences you will experience when you move ahead of God's timing.

What techniques can you incorporate into your routine to help you stay patient?

Name some of the consequences we can suffer if we don't have patience.

Why is character important?

Define what character means to you.

How does one get appropriately trained in God's word?

How difficult is walking by faith, not sight (2 Cor 5:7)?

Do you have little, great, or perfect faith?

What steps will you take to get to perfect faith?

Are relationships or activities hindering your ability to reach this level?

Why can looks be deceiving?

True or False: Forgiveness does not guarantee access.

Should you forgive someone if they didn't ask?
What are the dangers of forgiving someone who did not ask you for forgiveness?

Why do people fall into the trap of automatically forgiving someone who did not ask for forgiveness?

How can you demonstrate self-control?

Why should we pray for wisdom?

Describe battles that you should fight or ignore.

How does be ye angry and sin not apply to you? Eph 4:26

True or False: You should forgive someone who has not asked for forgiveness.

What does courage look like to you?

Describe the characteristics and behavior of a real leader.

How will you prioritize God in your schedule?

Do you believe you are the exception to God's rules?

How will failing to gain the attributes of Christ hurt you?

Chapter 7

Who are the Single Avenue Residents who failed to reach their potential?

How did each one of them fail to live up to their potential?

Why do we experience a delay in our blessings?

What delays are you currently experiencing in your life?

Do you sometimes feel invisible?

If so, when and why do you feel this way?

Why do we feel restless?

True or False: Singleness is a disease that needs to be cured.

Why do some women resort to unsavory methods to get what they want?

What dangers do we face when we go after what we want without consulting God?

True or False: I'd rather be happy and single than married and miserable.

What goals are you striving for that are preventing you from growing in grace?

What are the consequences of focusing on what we lack?

Why should we not allow our emotions to guide us?

True or False: Satan can take away our blessings.

What blessings have you unintentionally given Satan permission to take away from you?

Read Prov. 18:21. Life and death are in the power of the tongue. What does this mean to you?

Are you speaking positive or negative words in your life?

What happens when you skip the growth process?

Do you pray fervently? If not, why not?

What role does community play in your quest to live an extraordinary life?

What lessons did you learn from Hagar?

What lessons did you learn from Tamar?

What lessons did you learn from Leah?

Chapter 8

When you're consistent, you grow in grace. Are you consistent?

What is false confidence? How can we fix this situation?

Who had the title of a prophetess?

What is Miriam most famous for in history?

How do you feel about hearing the word no?

Name the experiences when God said 'no' that you later realized were blessings.

Why does God say no to us?

Name three requests for which you are seeking God's response.

Name three ways in which God can answer our request.

How did you react when God says no or not yet?

True or False: No can be a blessing in disguise.

Why should we embrace saying no?

Describe Ruth and Naomi's relationship.

What decision(s) have you made that changed the trajectory of your life?

How do you approach your situation when you experience a fork in the road?

What obstacles has Satan placed in your life to cause chaos and confusion?

How will you approach resolving this situation?

How can you encourage someone?

Did Esther have a healthy marriage?

Why was Esther hesitant to entertain Mordecai's request to alert King Xerxes of Haman's plans to destroy the Jews?

What are your gallows?

What are people constantly using to try to deter you from your dream?

Not everyone is meant to join you on your journey. Who should you keep? Who should you remove?

What lessons have you learned from Miriam?

What lessons have you learned from Ruth?

What lessons have you learned from Naomi?

Chapter 9

Who are the Single Avenue residents who made the most of their bad hand?

How can you make the most of your bad hand?

What advantages are there to being single?

How did Rahab save her family?

Fill in the blank.

_____is something sorely lacking in our society. Do you agree?

Fill in the blank.

_____starts now. Do you agree?

Does your lifestyle reflect behavior that God will allow you to live in heaven with Him, or will you allow your stubborn, rebellious nature to sentence you to hell?

True or False: Your actions on earth will determine your residency in eternity.

What is a married single?

Name some famous married single women in the Bible.

What are some lessons that we can learn from married, single women?

True or False: No one can make you happy.

Why should we learn from others' mistakes?

What lessons can we learn from Rahab, Abigail, and Jepthah's daughter?

Chapter 10

What single avenue resident lived their lives like it is golden?

What does it mean to bloom where you are planted?

Describe Martha and Mary.

Why do we allow our sensible side to win over faith?

How can we be unapologetic like Mary?

True or False: God plans to bring us through the storm.

How can we show Christ our gratitude?

What does it look like to live life on offense?

Name five ways people attempt to steal your joy.

Why do people criticize you?

How do you deal with criticism?

What is a healthy boundary?

How can you create healthy boundaries?

How will you enforce your boundaries?

How do people react when you enforce your boundaries?

Time is a scarce resource. What does this mean to you?

If you're everything to everyone, then you risk being no one.~LaTosha Johnson
What does this mean to you? How can you apply this to your life?

How will you amplify this concept in your life?

Why do people resort to passive-aggressive behavior?

How will you react when someone is passive-aggressive towards you?

How should you respond to this behavior?

What does it mean to bless someone's mess?

What mess have you refused to bless?

Why don't some people celebrate our wins?

If you suspect that someone is trying to steal your sparkle, how should you react?

Jesus taught us to fight our battles by using God's word. How do you use his word to fight your battles?

Why do women struggle to advocate for themselves?

Read Matt. 10:16. What does being as wise as a serpent and harmless as a dove mean?

What lessons have you learned from Mary, Martha, and Jesus?

Chapter 11

Name the Single Avenue residents who left a legacy.

Fill in the blanks.

Christ showed us on more than one occasion that it's okay to _____spaces where you are not wanted (Matthew 13:58). He showed us how we are to _____ our bodies as temples (Matt 10:28, 1 Cor. 6:12-20, 2 Tim 2:22, 1 Thes. 4:3-5). He showed us how to _____ (Gal. 5:19-21, i.e., not to get drunk, not to have sex outside of marriage).

How has your life impacted the lives of those around you?

Why is it difficult to live with a selfish mentality?

Are there idols (people, things, activities) in your life?

What helps you to readjust your focus to Christ?

What are some things in which we misplace our faith?

Where should people go to seek validation?

Why do people fail to seek validation from God?

Focus on the Source and not the resource. How can you demonstrate this concept in your life?

Fill in the blank.
With God _ _ _ _, things are possible. (Matt. 19:26) Name experiences in how you have seen God achieve the impossible.

If you had the unique chance to interrupt your funeral, who would be there to mourn you?

Would there be any evidence of how you used your God-given gifts to impact and uplift other people's lives?

When you look around, are you overwhelmed by the number of lives you touched, or are you disappointed because you realize you failed to prioritize the things that mattered most in your life?

What area(s) of your life are you lacking spiritually?

What will you bring to the altar to express your faith that God will provide for your needs?

What lessons have you learned from Dorcas and the widows we discussed in this chapter?

Chapter 12

What gifts are you willing to analyze, apply, and your gifts?

Are you relying on your 9 to 5 as your sole source of income?

How should you view your nine-to-five job?

Do you believe relying on a 9 to 5 is a risk?

If so, what are you doing to diversify your income?

Why is it easy to drift away from God on the job?

How do you live out Col 3:23 verse in your job?

How do you deal with difficult people on the job?

What expectations have people projected onto you?

How should you react when someone attempts to project a label/stereotype onto you?

How can you prepare for the obstacles you will face in the corporate world?

How do you set boundaries at work?

What are some concerns in considering your coworkers like family?

How can you be as bold as a lion?

What is doormat behavior?

What are some questions to ask yourself when dealing with difficult people?

What principles should you keep in mind to boost your confidence on the job?

What Goliath have you faced? What Goliath are you currently facing?

What lessons can we learn from Daniel?

What principles do you need to remember that will help give you the confidence to confront someone?

How do you advocate for yourself on the job?

Is it wrong to negotiate your salary?

What examples do we have in the Bible of people negotiating with God?

What skills will you learn?

How will you gain these new skills?

What does Prov. 11:25 mean to you? How does this apply to your life? How can you use your skills to amplify your life?

Chapter 13

How will you make sure your dash is meaningful?

Living an extraordinary life does not happen by accident. It starts with being intentional about what you consume—spiritually, mentally, physically, emotionally, and financially. How will you be intentional?

Why do you believe Apostle Paul stated that being single is easier than being married?

"Imagination is everything. It is the preview of life's coming attractions," by Albert Einstein. How does your imagination affect your life?

What do the "previews" look like for your upcoming attractions?

Who influences your life?

What emotions typically dominate your previews?

What is the acronym for SINGLE?

What makes you unique?

What prevents you from discovering or cultivating your God-given gift?

How will you invest in yourself?

How will you find opportunities to use your gift?

How can you surround yourself with people who will encourage you to use your gift?

How will you scale your gift so it benefits the most people in the least amount of time?

What does lift as we climb mean to you?

Why is it imperative to lift as we climb?

How should you respond when someone wants to know why you are single?

Notes

Notes

Notes

Notes

Notes

Notes

Notes

Notes

Notes

Notes

Notes

Notes

Notes

Notes

Notes

Notes

Notes

Notes

Notes